science
museum

How to be a
vet

Amanda Li

Illustrated by
Mike Phillips

MACMILLAN
CHILDREN'S BOOKS

First published 2007 by Macmillan Children's Books
a division of Macmillan Publishers Limited
20 New Wharf Road, London N1 9RR
Basingstoke and Oxford
www.panmacmillan.com

Associated companies throughout the world

ISBN: 978-0-230-01543-2

Text design by John Fordham

Printed and bound in China

Picture credits:
Science Museum / Science & Society Picture Library Page 11
The Royal Veterinary College All other pictures

**The Royal Veterinary College
(RVC)** is the UK's first and largest
veterinary school and a constituent
college of the University of London.

The RVC offers a range of
undergraduate and postgraduate
degrees and short courses in the
veterinary field. The college is
also one of the leading veterinary
research centres in Europe and
received 5 out of 5 in the latest
Research Assessment Exercise. It
provides support for the veterinary
profession through its three referral
hospitals, diagnostic services
and continuing professional
development courses.

The college is based on two main
campuses, the Camden campus in
London and the Hawkshead campus
in Hertfordshire.

www.rvc.ac.uk

Contents

So, you want to be a vet?

Does being a real-life Dr Dolittle appeal to you? Working with animals and helping them to keep healthy and well sounds like a fascinating job. But being a vet is also very challenging – and very hard work.

VETS WANTED!

- Are you passionate about animals? ✓
- Are you prepared to work long hours, evenings and weekends? ✓
- Are you good at communicating with people? ✓
- Are you patient and sympathetic? ✓
- Do science subjects interest you? ✓

**Then you might just have what
it takes to become a vet.**

'**Vet**' is short for **veterinary surgeon**, a person who is qualified to diagnose, treat and prevent disease in animals.

Gill Forster is a vet who works at a small-animal hospital. She loves her job:

'I really enjoy working with animals and I also love talking to their owners. Probably the best thing about being a vet is the variety of the work. I never know what I'm going to encounter, and even after fourteen years I see new things every day. Performing surgery is one of the most challenging aspects of the job, and there is a great sense of achievement when things go well.'

Get set to be a vet

To become a fully qualified vet like Gill, you'll have to study hard to earn a place at **university**. You will need GCSE A levels in at least three science subjects, including Chemistry and Biology. Practical experience of working with animals is important so most students will have already spent time at a farm, stables or in a vet's practice.

If you're accepted, you'll spend five years studying for a degree in **Veterinary Medicine**. During this time you'll:

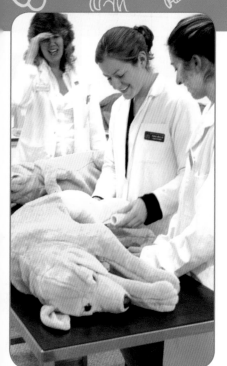

Veterinary students practising their bandaging skills on a dog model

- Learn all about the structure and function of animals' bodies and their diseases and treatments.
- Get practical experience during placements at farms, stables and animal hospitals.
- Do clinical studies and lab work.
- Develop business skills that will help you in the future.

If you pass your degree, you'll need to get registered as a **Member of the Royal College of Veterinary Surgeons**. Then, finally, you'll be able to start work as a vet!

creature feature

One of the tasks that vets do is microchipping. A microchip is a tiny capsule, about the size of a grain of rice, which the vet can quickly and easily insert under the animal's skin. It contains a unique identification number that will help a pet's owner find their pet if it is lost.

A day in the life of a vet

Vets usually work in veterinary surgeries (also called practices) or in animal hospitals. Animal charities such as the RSPCA, animal-rescue centres, wildlife parks and zoos also employ vets.

Which kind of animal?

Surgeries vary in size and specialize in different kinds of animal – some handle only small animals, such as cats and dogs, while others treat larger animals, such as cows and horses. Whichever kind, an appointment (called a **consultation**) must be made with the vet by the animal's owner. For small animals, these consultations take place at the vet's surgery.

What's the problem?

The owner talks to the vet to explain why they have brought their animal in. It might be just for a routine health check or vaccination, or there may be a more serious problem that needs investigation. If this is the case, the vet needs to examine the creature to find out as much as possible. Computer records will also show details of the animal's medical history.

Veterinary nurses are a very important part of the veterinary team

A vet's day

Because a vet's work varies so much there's no such thing as a typical day. Here is just one day in the life of small-animal vet Gill Forster. The surgery she works for has branches in different areas.

9 a.m. Arrived at work at the branch surgery. Consultations until 11 a.m. Saw lots of animals and their owners, including a kitten that had come in for a general health check. Treated a puppy that had been hit by a car – luckily he only had a grazed leg.

11 a.m. Back to the main practice. Checked on patients from the previous weekend, when I was on duty. Then performed two hours of surgery, including a cat spay (removing the ovaries so the cat can't have kittens). I changed the dressing on a dog with a broken leg and X-rayed another dog.

1 p.m. Break for lunch.

1.30–3.30 p.m. More consultations. Saw a Great Dane with lumps under the skin and booked him in for an operation later in the week. Did vaccinations and checked a cat with a mouth problem, giving dental advice.

4–5 p.m. Caught up on letters and phone calls, checked lab results.

5–7.30 p.m. Consultations at another branch.

creature feature

As a small-animal vet, Gill mainly treats dogs, cats and rabbits. Other creatures that she sometimes sees are guinea pigs, ferrets, mice, rats, birds, chinchillas, hamsters, chickens, lizards and snakes.

The veterinary nurse

It isn't only the vet who helps animals and gives them medical treatment. Veterinary nurses work alongside vets and they can do many of the tasks that vets perform.

Becoming a veterinary nurse

Just like a vet, you must be an animal lover who is prepared to study hard and work long hours. At school you will need to pass five GCSE exams, including English, Maths and a science subject such as Biology. (Or you can take a one-year Animal Nursing Auxiliary qualification.) The next step is to go to college as a student veterinary nurse, learning how to care for and nurse animals, perform simple surgical techniques, radiology (X-rays), and about pharmacology (medicines) and many other animal-related subjects. There will be lots of opportunities to practise your new skills while being supervised by a qualified vet. The course takes two years.

A qualified veterinary nurse can perform the following tasks:

- Consultations with animals and owners, including health checks.
- Changing dresses, removing sutures (stitches) and staples from animals who are recovering after operations.
- Giving medication.
- Nursing animal patients.
- Lab tests and taking blood samples.
- Taking X-rays.
- Assisting before and during surgery.

creature feature

Cats tend to suffer from abscesses — nasty build-ups of pus and other fluids — that may lead to more serious infections. The reason for this is that cats often get into fights. As their teeth and claws are covered in bacteria, any wound can easily develop into an abscess and a visit to the vet may be needed. The veterinary nurse will probably drain the fluid out through a small cut and prescribe antibiotics, which fight infection.

Holly Field is a veterinary nurse who works at a large small-animal referral hospital.

'I really love my job as a veterinary nurse because I can spend time with the animals, getting to know them and giving them the care they need to recover from illness. It is enormously rewarding when I have played a big part in a patient's recovery and get to see them go home with their owners happy!'

Closing a wound using sutures

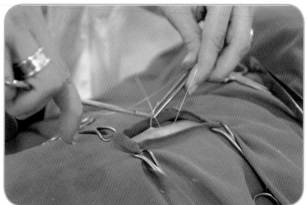

The 'surgeon' nurse

Veterinary nurses are allowed to perform simple surgery on animals – anything that does not involve entering the body cavity. So, as a nurse, you could find yourself in the operating theatre stitching up a small wound or perhaps removing a growth from under the skin.

A veterinarian and two veterinary nurses working together to perform a check-up

Treating animals in the past

Throughout history people have lived and worked with animals, depending on them for their livelihood and caring for them in the best way they could.

People in the past had very little scientific knowledge when it came to animal health and anatomy (the structure of animals' bodies), and creatures were treated according to ancient traditions and customs. Writings have been found from ancient China, Rome and Greece about caring for animals. One Roman writer called **Cato** described how a mixture of olive oil and wine was a good treatment for something called 'sheep scab'!

Bleeding beasts

One of the old-fashioned ways of treating animals – and humans too - was **bloodletting**, as for hundreds of years it was thought that letting blood escape from the veins was good for the health. Horses were bled regularly.
A small incision would be made in the jugular vein, which runs down the side of the neck, and the spurting blood was collected in cups. It all sounds strange to us now, but at the time people firmly believed that they were doing good.

Old-fashioned surgical instruments

The farrier

One of the people that used to perform bloodletting was the **farrier**. This is a person who fits horseshoes – iron plates that are nailed to horses' hoofs to protect them. The farrier had no proper medical knowledge but treated horses long before the existence of vets.

The farrier's guide to giving medicine to a horse

1. The 'medicine' comes in the form of a very large pill and it tastes revolting. The horse is **not** going to like it.

2. Restrain the horse so that it doesn't rear up or gallop off.

3. Place the pill in the balling gun. This is a long wooden device that is specially designed to get pills into reluctant animals.

4. Put the balling gun in the horse's mouth and eject the pill at the back of the throat. **Down it goes!**

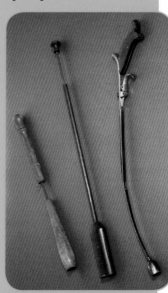

Three different types of balling gun

creature feature

Throughout history people have been able to estimate the age of horses by looking at the shape, angle and appearance of their teeth. They also count the number of permanent teeth that younger horses have.

These days, vets can use hypodermic syringes to inject drugs directly into a sick animal. But balling guns are still used by vets if a creature has to swallow a pill, although nowadays they are made from steel.

11

The rise of the horse doctor

Over many years veterinary medicine has developed into the respected science it is today. Much of this progress happened because of one creature: the horse.

The horse in history

It is not really surprising that many animal medical treatments from the past are concerned with horses. Horses have been incredibly important creatures to humans throughout history. They have carried us on their back, pulled our carts and carriages and laboured on our farms. Before the invention of the motor car, horses were our main form of transport, taking us practically everywhere – even into war.

War horse

For many hundred of years horses were ridden into battle and were also used to pull guns and transport ammunition for armies. The need for proper horse doctors eventually became so great that in 1796 the Army Veterinary Service was founded. These army vets were trained at the London Veterinary College and were then sent to attend injured horses on the battlefield. In fact, many advances in animal medicine were made during wartime.

The first schools

Over the years, various texts had been written about animal care, but there were no schools in existence until 1761, when the very first school of animal medicine was opened in France. Similar schools soon followed in other European countries, including England.

Veterinary students help the vets look at a horse's breathing

Eclipse's statue, on display at the RVC

Eclipse – an inspirational horse

Eclipse was a beautiful champion racehorse that won many races in 1769 and 1770. After Eclipse's death a Frenchman called **Charles Benoit Vial de St Bel** wanted to find out the secret of the horse's success, so he examined Eclipse's body in detail, writing long reports on his findings. This work made him realize that a better understanding of animals was needed. So, with the help of an agricultural society, he established the **London Veterinary College** in 1791. It started off as a London hospital specializing in horses, but gradually grew in size and reputation and was eventually granted a Royal Charter in 1875. It is now called the **Royal Veterinary College** (RVC). Today the RVC is known and respected all over the world and trains hundreds of students to become top-class veterinarians, nurses and scientists, treating all kinds of animal.

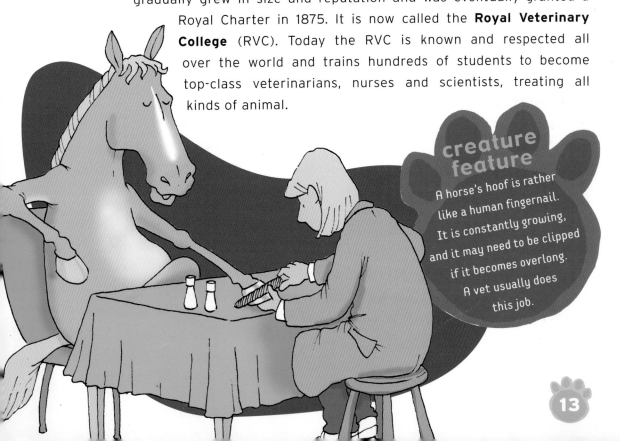

creature feature

A horse's hoof is rather like a human fingernail. It is constantly growing, and it may need to be clipped if it becomes overlong. A vet usually does this job.

The modern vet's surgery

Our knowledge of animals has increased hugely in the last hundred years. Modern-day vets are lucky to have information at their fingertips and the latest equipment to use in their work.

Making a diagnosis

During the consultation with the owner, the vet needs to find out exactly what is wrong with the animal. This is called a diagnosis. Talking to the owner about the animal's symptoms and examining the creature help the vet get a better idea of what the problem might be. He or she might also:

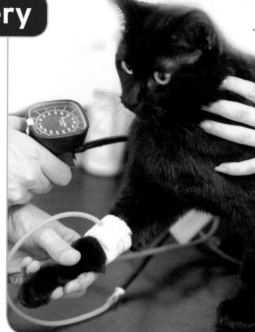

Monitoring blood pressure

- Listen to the animal's **heartbeat** – the vet will use a stethoscope to see if the heartbeat is normal.

- Take the animal's **temperature** – the vet will use a thermometer for this.

- Take an **X-ray** – a special photograph that allows the vet to see right inside the animal. X-rays can be used to confirm suspected broken or fractured bones or to see objects that may have been accidentally swallowed by the animal.

Checking for broken bones

- Do a **blood test** – the vet may take a sample of blood from the animal using a syringe. This will be tested in the lab for any suspected problems.

Treating the animal

Once the vet has diagnosed the problem, the animal's **treatment** can begin. Medicines may be prescribed and, if the animal has an infection, a type of drug called an **antibiotic** may be used, as it is very effective against bacteria. Wounds or broken limbs will need to be dressed or may be operated on and then set in plaster. There are treatments available for many different problems.

Preparing for an overnight stay

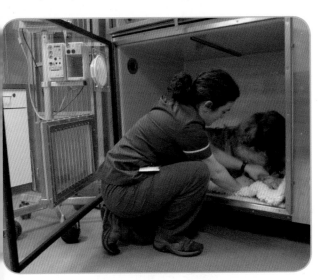

Vets will try not to keep animals in **overnight** unless they feel it is absolutely necessary, but most practices have space for observing and treating smaller animals. Larger hospitals may be able to keep animals such as horses. If an animal stays at the surgery or hospital, it will be put into a safe cage or pen. A treatment chart will be filled in regularly by the vet or nurse. This shows any medication the animal is receiving and when it was last given.

creature feature

Vets recently performed emergency surgery to remove an object from the stomach of a Staffordshire bull terrier. The X-ray showed that the puppy had swallowed a 26-centimetre-long tent peg.

Vets and pets

If you work for a small-animal hospital, you will usually be treating cats and dogs. Here are the most common procedures that you will be performing:

- **Vaccinations**

  Pets can be **vaccinated** for protection against certain diseases, just like humans. The vet uses a syringe to inject a liquid called a vaccine directly into the animal. The vaccine contains a harmless form of the disease and it will prevent the animal from ever catching it in the future.

Pets are usually vaccinated at a young age – puppies at eight weeks and then again at twelve weeks. This will prevent them getting canine diseases such as distemper and parvovirus. Kittens are vaccinated at nine and twelve weeks against viruses such as cat flu. Rabbits may also be vaccinated, against diseases like myxomatosis.

Neutering a cat

- **Neutering**

  Vets will often perform an operation called **neutering** on cats and dogs to prevent them from having babies. The pet is given an **anaesthetic** to make sure that it doesn't feel any pain during the surgery, and their stitches are taken out after about ten days. In male pets this operation is sometimes called castration, and in female pets, spaying. It is not at all cruel as the animal will lead a longer, healthier life and may even be prevented from catching some diseases. It also means that there will not be lots of unwanted kittens and puppies around with no one to care for them.

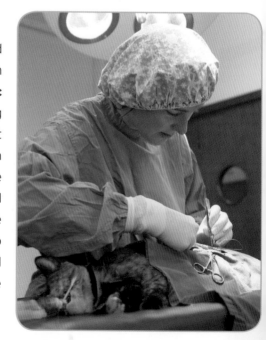

• Dental work

Vets do a lot of dental work and will often give owners advice about caring for their pets' teeth. Animals' teeth are very important and many illnesses can be avoided if they are properly looked after. For example, a substance called tartar can build up on the teeth, causing a nasty infection. Vets can remove this tartar, but it is even better for the owner to prevent it building up in the first place by cleaning their pets' teeth regularly. Special toothpastes are now available for animals – fish toothpaste is especially popular with cats!

Vets may also file down the teeth of small mammals such as rabbits.

• Health checks

Vets and veterinary nurses can carry out general health checks on pets, giving advice on all the above subjects, as well as other important issues, from worming to flea control, diet to behaviour.

creature feature

Rabbits' teeth never stop growing. This is because their diet contains a lot of grass and hay and constant chewing is required. Overgrown teeth can cause problems for some domestic rabbits and this is why they may need to be filed by the vet.

Unusual pets

Sick snakes and lethargic
lizards may occasionally
make an appearance at
a vet's surgery. Creatures
like these have usually been
imported from other countries and
they need special care.

Educating the owners

Many of the problems that vets see in exotic pets are caused by their
owners, who don't know enough about their pet. Some creatures
are being fed the wrong kind of diet or are being kept in an
unsuitable environment. Many exotic pets need special equipment
such as vivariums (an indoor enclosure for keeping animals under
natural conditions) and heat lamps, which the vet can give advice on.

Some exotic-pet problems

- **Snakes** can often harbour parasites – tiny ticks or mites, sometimes
  no bigger than a pinhead, which live under the scales of the skin. If
  left untreated these creatures can make the snake very ill. New snakes
  should be checked by a vet to make sure they are clear, then regularly
  inspected by their owner.

- One of the illnesses that can
  affect caged **birds** is zinc
  poisoning, which may happen
  if a bird is put into an unsafe
  cage. A vet can advise on
  this and can also treat birds
  suffering from metal poisoning.

Vets care for lots of different
and unusual animals

Feeding antibiotics to a gecko

- **Lizards** and other reptiles may suffer from respiratory infections, causing wheezing, gurgling and bubbling from the mouth and nose. The usual cause is the lizard not being warm enough, so the heat levels in its vivarium will need to be increased. However, if the infection persists, the vet may need to prescribe antibiotics.

creature feature

It may come as a surprise to know that the humble guinea pig is classified as an exotic pet, along with many types of lizards, snakes, birds and spiders. An exotic pet is any creature that does not come from the United Kingdom. Guinea pigs originally came from Peru.

Sick spiders and ... superglue?

Heard the one about the spider that got superglued? It may sound like a joke, but in real life a vet did exactly this. The patient was a large hairy tarantula that had damaged its exoskeleton in a fall. Hemolymph – the spider's equivalent of blood – was leaking out and the tarantula would have died if it had lost too much. However, a speedy application of superglue to the wound by a quick-thinking vet meant that the creature made a full recovery.

Something wild

Injured wild creatures are sometimes found by people and brought to a vet's surgery for treatment. They need to be cared for in a special way.

A different approach

Creatures such as **badgers**, **wild rabbits**, **foxes**, **hedgehogs** and **wild birds** are not always the easiest of patients to treat. Unlike cats and dogs, who are used to people and may be comforted by petting, wild animals will usually be very frightened of humans. Vets know that they should be handled as little as possible; otherwise they will become very stressed and may not respond well to treatment.

Students learn about how to properly feed and house chickens on a farm

Causes of injury

Many of the injuries that vets see in wild creatures are caused by:

- Road accidents.
- Attacks by other animals, sometimes cats and dogs.
- Being caught in traps or snares.
- Being poisoned by substances humans have used on crops or in gardens, e.g. pesticides. Even slug pellets can kill hedgehogs or birds.

Bird problems

Wild birds such as **swans** can get tangled up in discarded fishing tackle or they may be poisoned if they swallow the lead weights used by fishermen. **Oil spillages** from ships can also cause terrible problems for birds, as the sticky oil removes the waterproofing from their feathers and is poisonous when swallowed. Special cleaning is needed.

Hedgehog harm

Hedgehogs like to hide themselves in gardens, so they are often brought to the vet by people who have accidentally injured them while mowing the lawn. Hedgehogs also like to take shelter in bonfires and compost heaps so they should be checked before lighting or raking.

creature feature

It's a sad fact that more than five million wild creatures in Britain are injured every year by dangers created by humans.

Treatment and beyond

Recovering animals should be returned to the wild as soon as possible. In one case, a young **badger** suffered a broken leg and jaw in a car accident. The vet operated on both and the creature made a full recovery. It was soon returned to its set – the badger's natural home.

Sometimes, however, an animal can no longer survive in its natural environment. This was the case when a **snowy owl** was found on an air-force runway a few years ago with its right wing completely torn off, probably due to a collision with a plane. The owl's wound was dressed and it soon recovered, but with only one wing it would never again be able to hunt for food. Fortunately a home was found for him in a large aviary, where he is now living happily.

On the farm

As a vet you can choose to specialize in small or large animals. If you work with large animals, you will spend much of your time visiting farms, as your patients cannot easily be brought into the surgery.

The farm vet

You will be dealing mainly with **cows**, **pigs**, **sheep** and **horses** and may be called out at any time of the day or night to deal with medical emergencies or to help with animals giving birth. The vet gives vaccinations against diseases such as tetanus and will give the farmer advice on feeding, breeding, worming and general care. Two important parts of the job are **preventative medicine** (stopping illnesses from happening in the first place) and **disease control**.

Disease detective

Farm vets need to know all about the various illnesses that farm animals can get. This is very important because farm animals usually live together in large groups so diseases are quickly passed between creatures in a flock or herd. Because cows, pigs and sheep are eaten by humans, there may also be risks to human health from their diseases.

If there is a serious **outbreak**, other people need to get involved too. Experts in areas such as public health and infectious diseases will work together with the vet to investigate the disease and try to find the best way of treating and controlling it.

creature feature

A cow spends up to eight hours a day chewing the cud (partially digested food). It will also drink the equivalent of a bathtub of water every day.

A new disease

A disease called **BSE** (also known as **mad cow disease**) was first discovered in British cattle in 1986. BSE is a very serious illness that affects the brain and nervous system. At first scientists did not think that BSE could affect humans, but we now know this is not the case. Some people have developed a type of brain disease that may have come from eating infected meat. Farmers, vets, scientists and the government have been working together to prevent the disease spreading and to try to find a cure for BSE.

The zoo vet

Some vets decide to specialize in the care and management of wild animals. The work of a zoo vet is incredibly diverse – one day you could be dealing with a flock of flamingos, the next a groggy giraffe.

The role of the zoo vet

- **Inspection duties** - checking that animals kept in captivity are living in good conditions.
- **Prevention of illness** among animals and emergency care.
- **Breeding programmes** - modern zoos work to conserve animal species, and vets are needed to help the animals to breed.
- **Disease control** and research.

The day usually starts with the vet and other staff checking any sick animals to make sure there have been no problems overnight. Then the rounds begin, when the vet sees any new patients. The vet will talk to the zookeepers, who have expert knowledge of the animals they look after.

Vets can also specialize in wild-animal health, working in zoos all over the world, or even in African game parks

creature feature

You'd need to run if you wanted to keep up with a giraffe taking a walk. The giraffe's long legs enable it to take extremely long steps — each is more than four metres long.

Bruno gets a pedicure

Bruno, a male giraffe at Whipsnade Wild Animal Park, was suffering from a painful problem with his hoofs. Occasionally a giraffe's hoofs can grow too much, or in the wrong direction, which makes it difficult for it to walk. Bruno's hoofs were growing forward instead of downward so they needed to be trimmed. But how on earth do you clip the hoofs of a very large, very lively giraffe?

The answer: Bruno needed to be **anaesthetized**. However, this can be a risky business and a large animal like Bruno could easily injure himself as the anaesthetic started working, making him sleepy and groggy. To help protect him, the zookeepers lined the walls of the giraffe house with bales of hay in case he wobbled around and knocked himself. Bruno also had to have a tube inserted in his windpipe to stop any food from his stomach getting into his windpipe and lungs. The procedure involved a whole team of people, including veterinary staff, students and a specialist horse surgeon. However, the hoof trimming was a great success and Bruno was walking around quite happily just an hour later.

Performing an operation

As a fully trained vet you will often be in theatre performing surgery. This vet is about to operate on a dog that has had its leg broken in a road accident.

Before the operation

The vet and support staff must 'scrub up' before they start work. Hands and arms are thoroughly washed with special soap to get rid of any bacteria. The vet puts on a clean surgical gown, together with a cap, mask and gloves.

In the 'prep' room

Before surgery the animal patient must be fully prepared in a special room. Here, the nurse is responsible for giving 'pre-meds' (sedatives), a type of medicine that has a calming effect on the animal. Painkillers also need to be given. The animal is now ready to be anaesthetized by the vet so that it will be asleep during the operation.

A dog under anaesthetic

A vet says ...

'Fixing broken bones in dogs and cats can be very challenging - the bones can be tiny compared to yours or mine, making drilling holes and placing screws very fiddly! We can't tell a dog or a cat to rest its leg either!'

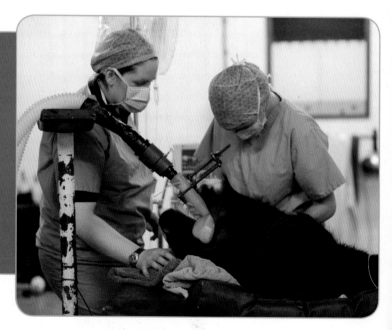

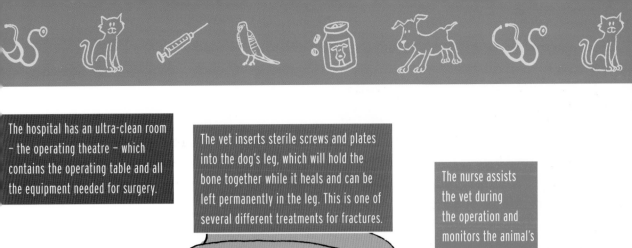

The hospital has an ultra-clean room – the operating theatre – which contains the operating table and all the equipment needed for surgery.

The vet inserts sterile screws and plates into the dog's leg, which will hold the bone together while it heals and can be left permanently in the leg. This is one of several different treatments for fractures.

The nurse assists the vet during the operation and monitors the animal's anaesthetic levels.

This machine displays the animal's anaesthetic levels.

This ventilator supports the animal's breathing during the operation.

The injured dog is covered in drapes, apart from the area to be operated on, which is left exposed. This area has been clipped and wiped or sprayed with antiseptic to avoid infection.

Some operations are observed by a student vet or nurse, who can learn a great deal from watching actual surgery taking place.

Sterilized steel instruments are used, such as a sharp scalpel for making the incision and special tweezers for gripping and pulling. After surgery the vet sutures (stitches) the wound up.

A variety of vets

There are so many different kinds of creature in the world, each with its own unique body structure, behaviour and lifestyle. And, as you now know, there are also many different kinds of vet.

What's your speciality?

Once you have qualified as a vet, there are many different types of animal you could learn more about. You could become an expert in, for example, wild-animal biology, exotic pets or equine medicine (the study and care of horses).

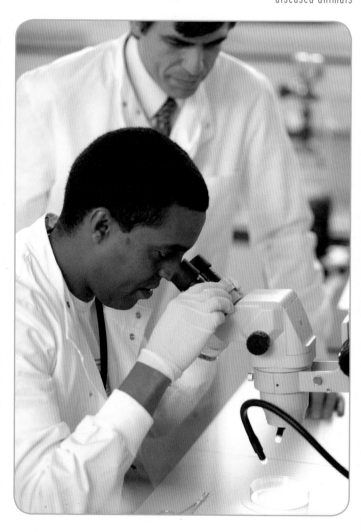

Veterinary scientists look at cells from diseased animals

There are also many vets who go on to specialize in other animal-related areas. Some of them do scientific research, spending time in the laboratory trying to find new ways to help animals and cure or prevent diseases. Some of the areas that you could specialize in are:

- **Musculoskeletal biology** – investigating the system of organs, muscles and bones that enable creatures to move.

- **Genes and reproduction** – exploring new ways of using genes – the building blocks of all life forms – to enable animals to have healthy babies.

- **Epidemiology** – the study of the causes and control of disease in animal populations.

In the modern world, scientific research into infection and disease has become very important. This is because new forms of disease have appeared over the years that could possibly be transmitted from animals to humans.

Avian flu

Avian flu – also known as **bird flu** – is a disease of birds. There are many different kinds (called 'strains') of bird flu, some of which spread very easily between birds, causing serious illness. In recent years some humans – mostly people who have been living very closely together with birds – have caught bird flu too. The disease is being very carefully monitored all over the world in case it turns into a strain that can easily be passed from person to person. A lot of research is being done, from monitoring and investigating the spread of bird flu to trying to find a drug that will cure it.

creature feature

Every year millions of birds leave their home to fly in search of a breeding area – a good place to lay eggs and raise their young. They also need to find food when the seasons change. This journey is called migration and some birds may cover huge distances of hundreds of kilometres. Scientists follow the paths of migrating birds to see where they are going. This is especially important for tracking diseases like bird flu, because migrating birds may take the disease to another part of the world.

An exciting future

As a vet you will be using the very latest technology and information available to the medical world. But this wasn't always the case.

Past times

Throughout history, advances in animal medicine have often lagged behind those made in human medicine. Instruments like thermometers and stethoscopes

were used by vets at a much later date than human doctors. And animal surgery was limited to just a few simple procedures until the late-nineteenth century.

Things are very different nowadays. Humans and animals sometimes suffer from the same diseases, so animals can often be given the same treatments. They too can be made better by powerful drugs like antibiotics or have the same kind of surgeries as humans, such as hip replacements. Indeed, some of the very latest developments in human medicine have been used to help animals.

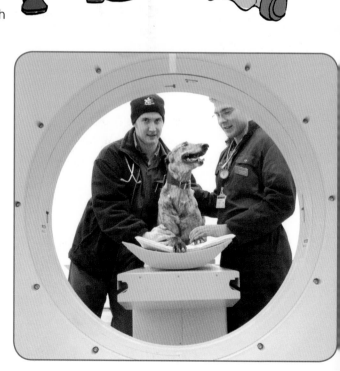

This dog is about to have a CT scan to look inside his body

Super stem cells

An injured racehorse called Zara has recently undergone a pioneering new treatment called **stem-cell therapy**. Stem cells are special cells that have the ability to divide and to become other types of cell. Scientists have discovered that they can be used to repair tissues in the body and even to grow new organs. This incredible discovery may one day revolutionize human and animal health, but the research still has a long way to go.

creature feature

A West Highland Terrier called Bonnie was suffering from problems with her heart. Vets performed surgery to insert a pacemaker, a small unit that helps regulate the heartbeat, under the skin of her neck. It is connected to the heart via a long lead. Years ago this operation was only performed on humans, but nowadays animals are able to have it too.

Zara's procedure involved collecting bone marrow – where the stem cells live – from inside her bones, using a long needle. The collected cells were then taken to the laboratory and multiplied many times, as millions of stem cells were needed for the treatment. When enough cells had been produced they were injected into Zara's damaged tendon (a tough band of tissue that connects a muscle with another part of the body). The aim is to help the tendon heal much more quickly and to make it very strong and flexible again. Zara is still recovering but her vet hopes she will one day return to the racetrack in excellent condition.

Whatever other exciting developments may happen in the future, one thing's for sure: whichever type of vet you choose to be, you will have one of the most interesting and satisfying jobs around.